Also by the author

Special Situations in Stocks and Bonds (1955)

How to Profit From Special Situations in the Stock Market (1959)

Fortunes in Special Situations in the Stock Market (1961)

Stock Market Profits Through Special Situations (1964)

Investor's Guide to Special Situations in the Stock Market (1966)

Special Situations in Securities

Maurece Schiller

Copyright © 1961, 1964, 1966 and 1970 Maurece Schiller

Copyright © 2018 Jill Schiller Bornstein and Donald J. Schiller

This article originally appeared in the 1964, 1966 and 1970 editions of the *Encylopedia of Stock Market Investing* (Larchmont: American Research Council and Larchmont: Investor's Intelligence) and was drawn from Schiller's *Fortunes in Special Situations in the Stock Market* (1961).

All rights reserved. Printed in the United States of America. Except as permitted under the United States Copyright Act of 1976, no part of this publication may be reproduced or distributed in any form or by any means, or stored in a data base or retrieval system, without prior written permission of the publisher.

This publication is designed to provide accurate and authoritative information in regard to the subject matter covered. It is sold with the understanding that neither the authors nor the publisher is engaged in rendering legal, accounting, investment or other professional service. If legal advice or other expert assistance is required, the services of a competent professional person should be sought.

Published by CreateSpace Independent Publishing Platform

The Marfa Group, Inc.
PO Box F
Marfa, TX 79843
(432) 203-2250

Book design by Susan Veach
Cover design by Ty Nowicki
Editorial assistance by Betsy Goolsby

ISBN-13: 978-1985134348
ISBN-10: 1985134349

Printed in The United States of America

INTRODUCTION

OUR GOAL IS to give guidance, information and understanding in special situations in the belief that comprehension of basic principles underlying special situation investing procedures will open a new field for investors.

By simplifying heretofore seemingly complex investing procedures, we introduce trading procedures for minimal risk work-out–type situations through the "something doing" group, offering substantial percentagewise return on money invested. We are guided by developments in a company's affairs that are identified by activities outside traditional business functions of the company. These administrative activities are responsible for endowing special situations with potentials for larger profits than are present in ordinary investments.

Of additional interest to investors is the broad use of trading procedures presented here, since they are not confined to new investment commitments. Not infrequently, securities holders are faced with a corporate event arising within a company whose securities they own. This might occur in any of the 10 corporate action arenas discussed herein, such as a tender, a merger, recapitalization, etc. Knowledge of trading venues open to securities holders in such circumstances could be most valuable and substantially broaden their investing range.

As we know, a business makes money in relation to management's "know-how"—the knowledge responsible for selecting proper procedures to do a specific job. Similarly, in securities the use of know-how can be the measure of potential success. Therefore, knowing the trading procedures outlined here—knowing what to look for, where to find it, and when to do it—will give know-how for making money in special situations.

I want to thank the American Research Council, Rye, N.Y., publisher of *Fortunes in Special Situations*, for their courteous permission to draw upon this book for reference.

Maurece Schiller

A TRUE SPECIAL situation reflects "something doing" within a company. This something doing is our guide and beacon for money making in special situation investing. Unlike ordinary investments, they have built-in moneymaking devices for assured profits—profits that can be mathematically calculated prior to investing. All the pertinent information available in the something-doing company supplies this valuable information.

There is nothing mystic or mysterious about special situations. They occur simply from an action springing from internal corporate events rather than at the business level. For example: when two companies merge, each has participated in the agreement to join forces. Profit potentials are found in price discrepancies arising from provisions of the merger.

Special situation investing is oriented toward capital gains, with profits developing independently of the trend of the securities market. For example: Occidental Petroleum announced plans for the acquisition of Hooker Chemical. Terms called for an exchange of 1/2 share of Occidental $3.60 preferred stock for each share of Hooker common. Each share of Occidental preferred would be convertible into 3 shares of Occidental common at any time. After stockholders of both companies had approved the acquisition, Occidental common was priced at $44 and Hooker at $61. Since the exchange terms permitted conversion of the new preferred into 1 1/2 shares of common, then the value of 1 Hooker share would be $44 x 1.5, equal to $66. This showed a spread, or potential profit, of 5 points, equivalent to $5 per share. Therefore, purchase of Hooker common and sale of Occidental common to be acquired through the exchange and conversion privilege would result in the calculated profit being achieved. Profit potentials in this situation were found in the price discrepancies arising from provisions of the merger.

The merger of Xerox and Ginn & Co. afforded a potential profit or spread of 13% subsequent to announcement of stockholders' approval of the merger plan. Terms called for each Ginn & Co. common to be exchanged for 0.1525 shares of Xerox. The latter was priced at $289.50 as compared with Ginn & Co.'s share price of $39.25. Thus, $289.50 x 0.1525 equals $44.15, equal to a spread of $4.90, or 11%. At the time the merger was publicly announced, Ginn was priced around $35 and Xerox at $279. This showed a spread of 17%.

Profit potentials in special situations cover a wide range of possibilities from minimal risk work-out–type investments, harboring large percentage-wise gains, through glamour situations where substantial capital appreciation reflects the dynamic power in bringing to light hidden assets. U.S. Smelting, Refining & Mining (NYSE) demonstrated this kind of action. The company owned substantial assets, but its shares did not reflect the appraised worth until an aggressive stockholder group actively pressed for action. Under new management and orientation, the shares rose from the low $20s to around the $100 level. Subsequent activities of the new group contributed to the stock's popularity as a market performer, thereby harboring trading opportunities reflecting mergers and acquisitions.

The four basic characteristics identifying special situations are:

1. A specific corporate event is evident.
2. The security (stock/bond) is available at a price below work-out or expected value. This is the discount status.
3. Availability of pertinent data supplies accurate measurable values. This makes it mathematically calculable.
4. Profits are not dependent upon securities markets trends.

When the corporate event happens, the profit has materialized. Special situations are found in the following corporate events:

1. Liquidations
2. Residual stubs
3. Tenders
4. Spin-offs
5. Appraisals
6. Oversubscriptions
7. Hedging/arbitrating
8. Mergers/acquisitions
9. Reorganizations
10. Recapitalizations

Special Situations in Securities

We have broadly described the field of special situations, emphasizing outstanding characteristics and areas where they may be found. We will study these individual categories and suitable trading procedures for each, but before doing so, we should examine some additional advantages that have significance for the investor.

Many special situations come within the scope of discount situations. To understand what is meant by *discount*, we take an example: a stock having an estimated work-out value of $40 a share and priced marketwise at $30 shows a discount of $10 a share, equal to a 25% discount from its expected worth.

In *discount situations*, the corporate event, or "something doing," either has or is likely to take place. Consequently, the anticipated value may be used to calculate the profit. This type of situation offers maximum safety while, in addition, unanticipated benefits frequently come to light, increasing profits substantially. Typical of this:

The Delaware & Hudson "situation," at the time consideration was given to whether the railroad should become part of the Norfolk & Western Railway system, offered a typical discount opportunity. The shares of D&H were priced around the $32 to $33 level, while the indicated minimum value, based on the Norfolk & Western offer was at the $41 to $42 level. This reflected sale of the railroad properties on terms equivalent to $0.41 a share of Norfolk & Western for each D&H common, while D&H would retain approximately $20.7 million in cash as well as a $15 million tax-loss carry-forward. Thus, the residual shell offered the potential of substantially greater value than the basic $41. At the time of the stockholders' meeting, when sale of the railroad properties was concluded, shareholders were advised that the residual company would be known as Champlain National and would immediately seek new, non-rail opportunities. Shortly thereafter, International Industries made an offer for Champlain of securities having an indicated value of $60 a share, which was subsequently sweetened to an offer equivalent to $62 a share in International Industries securities. The contemplated acquisition was reflected in Champlain shares moving to the $56 level. In this situation, we see that hidden values are plus values wherein true discount conditions are present. This became more evident with the entry of Foremost-McKesson into the picture with an offer of $50 market value of Foremost securities for each Champlain share.

An example of another situation harboring hidden values was disclosed in the LNC liquidation. At the time, the stock was priced around $7.50 a share. The indicated work-out value was estimated to be $11 to $12 a share. The company made three cash payments totaling $8.50 a share and also distributed Blue Ridge Real Estate units in the ratio of share for share.

This stock carried an indicated value for tax purposes of $2 a share. The Blue Ridge stock subsequently has risen to the $8.00 level, and moreover, the LNC residual stub has a small potential worth. This situation shows the significance of "hidden values."

Dividends on shares and interest on bonds, although important in ordinary investments, play a secondary or rather unimportant role in special situations. This advantage exists in response to emphasis being placed on the corporate event—the activity unrelated to the company's routine business for creation of profits. The impact of "something doing" establishes the special situation profit, since this is responsible for raising the market value of the securities to its calculated worth.

Since special situations are oriented toward capital gains, we can understand the advantage, under our present tax law, to have long-term capital gains (over 6 months) than receive a current return. Furthermore, many situations being work-out deals such as liquidations, where there are no earnings, would not be dividend- or interest-paying companies.

Despite dividends' unimportant role, the presence of dividends and interest often helps defray the cost of carrying a situation while awaiting developments. Viewed from this angle, special situation investors find it satisfying to participate in certain situations where "rumor" or only "informed rumor" represents the "something doing." This may happen where a recognized high-grade company is mentioned in association with a special situation category.

Another favorable feature in special situations is the somewhat automatic approach to buying and selling. On the buying side, "when to get in" can be answered by presence of our basic characteristics. If the fundamentals are in order, then the indicated profit will be a guide for participation. For example, if the situation shows a 20% potential profit and maximum time for consummation is two years hence, then rate of return would be 10%. In other words, if the situation is selling at an adequate discount from estimated value—buy.

When to sell is always perplexing to the investor in ordinary stocks and bonds; however, in special situations, when the "something doing," i.e., the activity arousing interest has consummated—get out. Consummation of the program often automatically terminates interest in the situation as occurs in a liquidation where the company pays each shareholder his proportionate share. In circumstances where an automatic out does not prevail, the policy of selling when the corporate event has taken place should be a basic rule. At that point, the calculated profit has been made.

In these automatic signaling characteristics of special situations, their relative immunity to outside influences is apparent. Because of this, special situation investors are not greatly concerned with the trend of securities markets.

Special situations offer, as an investment concept, a medium for increasing one's assets at a greater rate than the impact of inflation, thus, a logical avenue for investment. As we know, dollar erosion is a continual influence upon purchasing power. Since special situations are capital-gains oriented, then the successful corporate event will realize ultimate values and increase assets by that amount. In this way, we can buy profits to offset dollar erosion, since "something doing" is an internal activity not dependent upon the course of the securities market nor the national economy.

How to Estimate Potential Profit and Loss

While many special situations have the quality of minimum risk, it is important to carefully analyze the situation in bringing this about. Disclosure of hazards makes possible proper evaluation of the profits materializing. As important as it is to calculate profits, so is it vital to estimate loss possibilities. As we know, profits arise as a result of "something doing"; in view of this, we measure loss possibilities in relation to the extent of influence of the corporate event.

For example: Essex Wire and Cerro discussed merger possibilities. Since Essex would be the surviving company and a discount was indicated in the price of Cerro stock in relation to the proposed terms, our interest would be in Cerro common. The stock was priced around $42 at the time of merger discussions and had a low of $37.50 for the year. Terms of the merger called for each Cerro common to receive 0.225 shares of Essex common and 0.75 shares of new preferred, which would be convertible into one share of Essex. These terms, as you see, were equivalent to a share-for-share exchange. Since Essex was priced around $48, the indicated discount was 13%. Should the merger fail to consummate, then we could expect Cerro common to decline about 10%—just above the low of the year and around the price prior to merger discussions. Halting of the merger was reflected in Cerro's shares declining to $39.38.

In another example of a noncompleted merger involving Essex and Aerovox, shares of Aerovox reacted to the news by dropping from $18.75 to $14.38 and subsequently to around $13. The latter price was back to where it was selling prior to merger discussions.

It is advisable to check market action of the security somewhat prior to public announcement to see if anticipated buying has occurred. If the security has had a strong undertone immediately prior to public announcement, then the possibility of the security receding to that level should not go unrecognized. Where there has been earlier buying, knowing the position of such buyers in relation to "something doing" gives a clue to probable realization of the proposed plan. Buying by directors and officers of a company recommending a plan would support greater likelihood of the plan becoming effective as compared with early buying stimulated by unrelated purchasers.

Special Situations in Securities

We would not be considering the specific situation had we not already established the presence of corporate action and indicated undervalue, thus, we see that estimating profit potential is primarily an arithmetic step. This is particularly so in mergers/acquisitions and work-out situations. To illustrate: in a merger/acquisition, the initial approach is to figure the discount from the expected worth of the shares of the company to be absorbed. Such discount tells us how much can be made in dollars. In a tender invitation, we can readily figure the spread between market price and tender invitation price arithmetically, giving us the amount of the discount. In a liquidation, we mathematically calculate the per share distribution in the dissolving of the company.

In judging desirability of a situation, we view relationship of risk to profit potential. In work-out discount-type situations where dollar profits cannot be great, though percentage-wise return on money invested may be substantial, the probability of success must be high. With this in mind, we have found that situations showing an indicated gain of 10% on an annual basis should have about a 9 to 1 probability of success.

However, all special situations are not discount work-out deals. Consequently, financial analysis is helpful in both clarifying the situation as well as establishing confidence. To simplify the financial analytical approach, we have compiled a master set of pertinent questions designed solely for special situation analysis. Knowing the answers to these queries will decide participation and ways to estimate consummation of corporate action.

In addition to financial analysis, it is helpful to investigate favorable as well as unfavorable possibilities. For example: in a proposed liquidation, verification of dates for distribution of assets plays an important role. Since length of time capital is employed has a definite impact on rate of return on the investment, then obviously, verifying distribution dates by checking with the company could mean the difference between a profitable and unprofitable investment.

Corporate Analysis

When estimating probable realization of a proposed plan, the corporate set-up can be most revealing. Therefore, at this point we want to know:

5. The percentage of voting stock controlled by management, since this is the key to the likelihood of a plan being consummated. The information is found in the capital structure.
6. By perusing the charter provisions, we can find out *what percentage of outstanding shares* is required to vote affirmatively to assure consummation of the plan. The percentage of required affirmative votes to qualify a plan may range from a mere majority to as much as 90% or even 100% assent. Therefore, it is significant to know the minimum number of votes making a plan operative. The voting strength of larger holders who are in favor of the plan is generally obtainable from the company or disclosed in the Notice of Meeting. By relating the assured affirmative votes to the number essential to approve the corporation's move, we have a good indication of the ultimate result.
7. We would like to know if a significant number of shares is held by a cohesive group or is widely distributed. The answer to this is found in dispersion of the floating supply of shares. The stockholders' list will disclose this information. Widely distributed shareholdings generally cooperate with management's suggestions. On the other hand, a cohesive group could dominate the voting. This brings us to the subject of dissension.

Opposition to a Corporate Action

The significance of opposition to a corporate plan should not be minimized. To cover this aspect of the analytical approach, we have culled from the broad field of analysis pertinent factors affecting special situations. There follow significant questions where opposition is present, including caution signals such as:

Special Situations in Securities

1. Does opposition represent a single dissenter, a single group of dissenters, or is the opposition deep, stockholder-wise?
2. Upon what do the dissenters base their opposition? The quality of the claim may very well be disclosed in answer to this question.
3. What plan is offered by the opposition? Clarification of this point could be of material aid in making decisions about investing, since unwarranted risks may arise should the opposition win.
4. What is the position of government agencies? Recent activity on the part of the Department of Justice, Bureau of Internal Revenue (IRS), SEC, FCC, and ICC have broadened the area of possible opposition by government.

Sources of information about opposition to a corporate action can be found in newspapers, prospectuses, protective committees, dissident groups, and, of course, the Notice of Meeting & Proxy Statement.

The Analytical Approach

By combining financial analysis with investigation, we clarify profit potentials, risks, and attractiveness of the situation. The following short form of financial analysis, specifically designed for special situations, discloses essential data in viewing the financial picture. By applying the master list of queries to a recent balance sheet statement and earnings report, we learn the financial strength of the situation. The value of separating the analysis into two groups can be seen when we are studying mergers/acquisitions where sales, earnings, dividends, and profit margins are significant, whereas in liquidations and work-out situations, that information is bypassed for the more pertinent items such as cash, inventory, and working capital. You will recognize in Group I liquidation-type special situations and in Group II merger/acquisition and reorganization types.

MASTER FINANCIAL ANALYTICAL APPROACH

GROUP I

What is the cash position?

What is the inventory?

What is the working capital (per share)?

What is the book value (per share)?

What is the value placed on patents, goodwill, and intangibles? What are the reserves?

What are the contingent liabilities for taxes, legal matters and labor?

What is the established waiting period?

GROUP II

What are the earnings, net and per share?

What percentage of earnings is paid out as dividends?

What is the dollar volume of sales (gross)?

What is the dollar amount of sales per share of stock?

What is the percentage of profit on sales (profit margin)?

What is the gross and per share amount of taxes paid?

What is the long-term dividend record and, will dividends and interest be paid during the waiting period?

What is the ratio of each securities issue to the capitalization?

What are the depreciation and depletion charges?

What is the duration period for consideration of the proposed corporate action?

It is helpful to appraise the situation from the viewpoint of estimated worth of each corporation's shares. While in liquidations, a value may be indicated by the company; in other situations such as mergers/acquisitions, where more than one company may be involved, we may have to establish our own estimated values for the securities. For this we apply our financial analytical approach.

True special situations are not complex, although procedures for investing may be unfamiliar. The securities are of the general run of stocks and bonds traded on the various securities markets. Procedures for buying and selling follow similar lines common to other securities, with the significant difference in the *application* of securities trading procedures. Most investors are familiar with short selling merely as a broker's trading method. However, using short selling in an arbitrage/hedge situation or as a vehicle to establish a profit is an entirely new idea. In the following pages, we show how to use these trading procedures and short selling for profitable investing.

Sources of Information

We have discussed the various elements which, when combined in one investment, create a special situation. Sources that may disclose, add to, or validate information about these investments are the following: newspapers, financial news publications, advisory and statistical services, trade publications, libraries and the Securities & Exchange Commission (SEC). A most comprehensive and often illuminating source is the corporation itself through release of annual reports, interim reports, company organs, public relations releases, corporation officers' speeches, notices of annual meetings, prospectuses, reports to the SEC, and footnotes (the small-print section of company reports often include information and clues to values of properties and securities holdings).

In the foregoing, we have covered the broad spectrum of special situations showing capital gain potentials arising as a result of corporate action. We have discussed essential characteristics contributing to the making of a special situation. We have outlined the comprehensive master analytical approach for investing in these situations. Now we discuss each category and show by example (A) the basic nature of corporate action, (B) the origin of such situations, (C) specific methods for calculating potential profit, (D) the precise analytical approach, and (E) the trading procedures and how to apply them. We also highlight special information sources not included in our master analytical guide.

SPECIAL SITUATION TRADING PROCEDURES

A unique feature of special situations is in securities trading. Investing and making money can be accomplished through methods in "ways of buying and selling" securities. These situations are entirely independent of the company's business; in fact, opportunities arise because of discrepancies in prices of the same or equivalent securities.

We know in ordinary transactions when to buy, then wait for a rise in the securities, and when to sell. However, in special situation trading, we may buy and sell simultaneously (or as close as it is possible) to establish an arbitrage/hedge position. This procedure may be used in mergers/acquisitions, liquidations, reorganizations, oversubscriptions, and divestitures, as well as with convertible securities. The principles of securities trading procedures have been simplified for the general investor's use.

Let us look at arbitraging, an expression that may sound complex and unfamiliar. Is it really so? Were you in the produce business in New York, you might call your egg farmer in New Jersey for a price on his eggs; at the same time, you may have on your other phone a customer wanting to buy eggs. Since your customer will pay a higher price for the eggs than you would pay the New Jersey farmer, a price discrepancy is present. This affords opportunity to arbitrage because you buy in New Jersey and sell to your customer in New York. You have, in effect, simultaneously dealt in the same product in different markets and created a profit as a result of price differences. This same

Special Situations in Securities

principle is applied, with some variations, to securities. Arbitrage is then defined as transactions taking place simultaneously in corresponding securities in different markets or in identical securities in the same market.

General Telephone & Electronics' merger with Hawaiian Telephone presents a typical exchange of equivalent securities. Terms are provided for an exchange of common shares on a share-for-share basis. At the time the plan was announced, General Telephone was priced around $44.13 and Hawaiian Telephone at $39.63. This showed an arbitrage profit of 4 1/2 points. The procedure for obtaining the profit follows:

Sell short	100 General Telephone @ $44.13	$4,412.50
Buy	100 Hawaiian Telephone @ $39.63	(3,962.50)
	Gross profit	$450.00
	Indicated %	11.6%
	Net % profit	9.1%

After deducting commissions and documentary stamps, a net profit of $292 remains. Since the merger was consummated within four months and the profit percentage was 9%, the rate of return on money invested equaled 27%.

As we see, an important part of the transaction is the use of "short selling." Unlike ordinary trading, where short selling is generally thought of as the main aspect of the transaction, with attendant risks of market fluctuations, in special situations we make use of short selling much like one buys insurance as a protection against loss, as well as insuring the pre-calculated profit.

In the practice of special situation investing, short selling is associated with hedging, since the objective in that circumstance is to be on both sides of a fence at the same time.

"*Short*" means that at the time of sale, the seller is not in possession of the securities he has sold. The short seller expects to deliver the stock he has sold at a future date.

"Hedging" is taking a position in similar or equivalent securities designed to protect the investor against loss through compensatory price movements.

Technical Phases of Hedging

The physical borrowing of securities against a short sale, while a function of the broker, is the first checkpoint to ascertain whether shares are freely available for borrowing. Bear in mind that borrowed securities must be returned upon demand. Should the shares not be available, you would be forced to cover your short position, and the hedge position would be thrown out of balance.

Dividend dates of both securities in the hedge position should be checked in order to give proper recognition to the amount of the dividends to be paid. Should the hedge position be in a convertible bond, compare the interest received with the amount of the dividends to be paid out. When calculating your hedge position, remember that expenses include commissions plus federal and state documentary taxes.

Convertible Securities

Bonds and preferred stocks having convertible features offer a good medium for hedging. Bonds or preferred stocks having conversion privileges provide a greater degree of safety of principal and income than obtains in the common. Since the securities may be converted into the common, they offer participation in the growth of a company as well as sharing in the price rise of the stock at reduced risks. For example: If a preferred stock is convertible into three shares of common, then the preferred would rise three points for every one-point advance in the common, from the price level where the common would be at parity with the preferred. Parity would be the price where three shares of common would equal one share of preferred.

Sometimes the conversion privilege is not effective until a future date. In this circumstance, an opportunity to "hedge" may arise when trading has been initiated in the stock into which the convertible issue may be exchanged on a "when issued" basis. This prevailed in Studebaker preferred when it was possible to purchase the preferred stock and sell the common short "when issued" at a price sufficiently above the value of the preferred to warrant creating a hedge position. Then when the common was issued upon the conversion privilege being activated, the short position in the "when issued" securities was terminated by converting the Studebaker preferred into the equivalent number of common shares.

"When issued" or "when, as, and if issued" as a securities trading vehicle comes into being when trading is initiated prior to the time the securities are officially in existence. This trading may take place prior to a specific date of issue or in anticipation of a security to be issued. We discuss this aspect more fully later.

We may very well ask at this time why profit possibilities are present in the foregoing circumstances. The main reason, of course, is technical influences creating the price differences. Another reason is the ignorance or indifference on the part of the public.

Having discussed trading procedures, we now move ahead to specific special situations and begin with liquidations.

LIQUIDATIONS

Liquidations-type special situations are essentially capital gains investments offering minimal risk as well as potential for a substantial rate of return on the money invested. Liquidation of a company involves termination of business affairs, discharging debts, and distributing remaining assets to the shareholders. Unlike ordinary investments where earnings and dividends are basic, in liquidations we are primarily interested in asset values. This approach is the essence of capital gain orientation in liquidations.

For example: Delaware & Hudson presents a simple example where the company took on the complexion of a liquidation when the plan to sell the railroad properties to Norfolk & Western Railroad was approved. The indicated minimum expectation was $41 to $42 a share when the stock was priced around $32. This higher-than-market evaluation reflected the value of the 0.41 of a share of Norfolk & Western stock to be received for by each D&H share holder for the railroad properties. However, additional assets remaining in the shell included substantial cash and a tax-loss carry-forward of $15 million. The procedure for liquidation in this case involved a change of name of the residual company and a search for a profitable shelter for the residual assets. Two such havens came to the foreground, with offers suggesting values from $50 to $62 a share for each D&H share.

A detailed illustration of the liquidation procedure is found in the following: The Delhi Taylor Oil liquidation disclosed typical attractive possibilities for capital gain inherent in a liquidation work-out situation. We see how time or duration of employment of money plays a significant role upon rate of return on the investment. This element is often responsible for better-than-expected results in liquidations.

Delhi Taylor Oil's common stock was priced around $16 after having moved to this level in anticipation of a formal announcement of plans to liquidate. Estimated liquidating value in the early stages indicated a price in the low $20s. However, at the time liquidation was confirmed and a meeting date scheduled for stockholders to vote on the proposed liquidation, the shares had advanced to around the $23 level.

Investors' estimates of liquidation value had risen at this time and ranged from $25 to $27 a share. When the major liquidating distributions had been completed, stockholders received the equivalent of about $28.50 a share plus an interest in the residual assets of undetermined value, estimated from $1.00 to $2.00 a share.

This situation offered opportunity to purchase shares around $23.38 subsequent to the company's formal declaration to distribute $22 in cash along with rights to subscribe to Delhi Australian and distribution of Certificates of Participation in various other assets. This later stock subsequently became known as Delhi Contract Units. The package at this point had an estimated work-out value ranging from $28 to $30 a share.

Special Situations in Securities

Investor thinking at this stage followed the line that since a cash payment of $20 to $22 a share was a reasonable expectancy, then there would be only $2 to $4 a share invested in a residual having a value ranging from $8.50 to $10 a share. Investor risk at that point was minimal. Within six months, stockholders received the equivalent of $28.50 a share. This showed a profit of $5.12 a share, equivalent to 22% on money invested, or at a rate of 44%, since money was used for only 6 months. The simplicity of approach to this type of situation is brought into sharp focus in the following summary of investigatory steps prior to establishing an investment position.

Since the company had disclosed pertinent per share liquidating value and the Notice of Meeting divulged data about the bona fide stature of sale of assets, the remaining important point to be clarified was the stockholders' vote. Communication with the company indicated confidence that the required number of affirmative votes would be obtained since large holdings of insiders (officials and family) had indicated approval of the plan. Therefore, purchase of the stock was indicated.

Liquidations frequently work out better than the usual conservative estimate. As the liquidation progressed, we see in the foregoing that the estimated value rose from the low $20s at the initial stage to an indicated ultimate liquidating worth of around $30 a share.

Kinds of Liquidations

Liquidations vary in type as well as method of distributing assets. Best known, of course, is complete liquidation, wherein a company disposes of its assets at one time and distributes the proceeds of the sale to its stockholders. In the case of the Universal Consolidated Oil liquidation, the acquiring company paid the liquidating price directly to the stockholders. The procedure: a subsidiary company of Gulf Oil offered to purchase shares of Universal Consolidated Oil at $68 a share. Around the time of the offer, Universal Consolidated Oil shares were available at $64 a share. Since expected consummation of the plan was but a month hence, the situation appeared attractive in light of the indicated gross profit of 4 points. The transaction was completed as indicated, establishing a profit of $400 for each 100-share position, equal to a gross rate of return in excess of 70% since the situation had but one month waiting time.

A vital clue to special situation opportunities often arises from merely being aware of what to look for when scanning financial news. For example: Company X has been the subject of a liquidation type of situation. It was not ready for special situation action; nevertheless, progress was followed as it appeared in the news. One day the company announced provisions of a plan to liquidate. However, the stock at that time discounted this news and perhaps only a 10% potential profit was indicated. Knowing the percentage-wise significance of length of time our money is in use, we look for an indication (in news reports or by checking the company) for a schedule of distribution of assets. This is the significant clue. Should we find that a preponderance of our investment would be returned in a relatively short time, then the situation could be most attractive. This was evident in Universal Consolidated Oil and Delhi Taylor Oil.

Companies sometimes decide to partially liquidate thereby creating profit opportunities for special situation investors. The stamp of partial liquidation is sale of predominantly all of the operating facilities of a company. CKP Developments (formerly Cockshutt Farm Equipment) exemplifies this type of situation. Its liquidating procedure discloses a method for participation in order to make profit.

CKP sold substantially all of its farm equipment business to White Motor Co. CKP then had substantial cash, some facilities, and land holdings in Florida. Estimated values of remaining assets amounted to $25 a share. The stock was priced around $14 a share. Subsequent announcement by the company indicated cash received from sale to White Motor would be used to redeem 400,000 shares at $21 a share. Since substantial holders of CKP had indicated they would not offer their shares for sale, remaining holders would be sure of selling 40% of their holdings at the $21 price. In effect, this works out as follows:

Special Situations in Securities

Purchase 100 CKP @ $14		($1,400.00)
Sell to company 40 shares @ $21	Proceeds	840.00
Sell 60 shares @ market price $14	Proceeds	840.00
	Total proceeds	1,680.00
	Gross profit	$280.00

The 60 shares sold at the market represent the shares remaining after sale of the 40 to the company. These shares would be sold immediately upon notice from the company of the acceptance of stock at $21, thus closing the transaction.

Another liquidating procedure is the piecemeal way whereby operating assets are sold periodically and distributions to stockholders made accordingly. When LNC had been divested from Lehigh Coal and Navigation, it was understood that LNC would dispose of its assets over a period of time and liquidate. The shares were priced around $7.50 at the time of our interest. Estimated ultimate worth was $11.00 or $12.00 a share. Thus, a potential profit of $3.25 or $4.25 was indicated, equal to a return of 40% to 54%. However, the length of time one's money would be invested was not known. Nevertheless, the indicated 40% to 54% potential profit would show a return of 10% should distribution of the assets take as long as four years. The situation offered attraction for long-term capital gain.

Two years after the purchase of shares, the company distributed $5.00 a share. This return of capital reduced the investor's cost to $2.75 a share. Since the residual stock was priced at $6.00 a share in the market, the investor could sell his stock and establish a profit of $3.25 a share, equivalent to a rate of return of 20% over a two-year period. On the other hand, he could retain the shares awaiting further liquidating distributions. Since his investment would now amount to $2.75 a share and the stock was priced in excess of $6.00 a share, the potential for obtaining a greater-than-estimated liquidating worth is evident. This, combined with the lesser amount of money invested, increases the probability for a substantially higher rate of return. Based on cost as indicated above and market price, more than 100%

profit was apparent. Later developments brought additional cash distributions of $3.50, making a total of $8.50 in cash received. Then, to boot, the company distributed a share of Blue Ridge Real Estate units for each share of LNC held. This had an indicated value for tax calculations of $2.00 a share. However, as the stock seasoned a bit, it moved to the $8.00 level, adding substantially to the total value of the original LNC share. Moreover, the LNC stub has a residual, though small, value. We see in this situation that to date, $16.50 in value can be accounted for, plus a shade more from the stub.

There are times when a company offers its stockholders an option to get out. This circumstance comes about from a drastic change in the nature of the company's activities, usually attendant with disposal of some major assets. American Viscose utilized this type of liquidation. The following example shows the procedure.

AVC Corp. came into being as a result of American Viscose's sale of its operating facilities and eventual plan for liquidation. American Viscose had sold its plants to FMC and had $367 million to liquidate. Principal assets comprised cash and Monsanto Chemical stock. An additional asset represented by Certificates of Participation had a $9 million litigation review with the IRS for recoverable taxes.

A special situation opportunity arose around the time AVC announced an optional plan of liquidating: either to accept the exchange offer or to remain with AVC as an investment company. AVC's exchange offer comprised $35.44 in cash, 0.79 of a share of Monsanto Chemical, and a Certificate of Participation for each of its own shares. Since AVC shares were priced around $75 and the indicated work-out value of the package to be received in exchange was about $80.00 a share, a potential profit was indicated. This optional offer opened two channels for special situation investors, namely: (a) purchase of AVC and subsequent sale of all securities received in exchange, thereby establishing the full profit, and (b) sale of Monsanto Chemical stock then priced around $56.50 and retaining the Certificates of Participation. Since cash combined with proceeds from sale of Monsanto stock would show a profit of approximately

Special Situations in Securities

5 points, this procedure would create "stubs," i.e., Certificate of Participations, without cost. (See below: Procedure for Creating Stubs.)

What to Know About Liquidations

The indicated liquidating value of the liquidation company is the primary and most important item to know. In some instances, this information is stated by the company; at other times, we must do our own calculating. We apply our master analytical procedure with additional relevant facts such as:

1. How are assets or proceeds of sale to be distributed?
   This discloses whether cash or securities will be distributed. If securities are to be distributed, then it may be possible to insure the profit by selling short securities to be received.
2. How will one fare taxwise?
   This is generally clarified by the company.
3. How long is the duration period until liquidating distributions will be made?
   This indicates percentage return on investment; the earlier the cost is returned, the greater the percentage-wise profit.
4. Are hidden values a potential?
   Unexpected benefits are frequently uncovered in liquidations.
5. Has a reserve fund been setup to provide for claims arising from termination of production, warranties, legal contingencies, labor, and trade liabilities?
6. What is the quality of accounts receivable?
   This discloses whether estimated net asset value may be subject to adjustment for bad accounts.
7. How do legal aspects shape up?
   Not only should claims against the company be checked, but also added potentials to the indicated liquidating value. For example:

British Columbia Power, when in liquidation, had $19.30 (Canadian) indicated as a minimum expectancy. However, the company's suit, which developed after liquidation had become evident, resulted in a substantially greater amount being received by stockholders.

Thus, when stock was purchased under $19.30, then the legal aspect was included at no cost to the investor.

Information about a liquidating situation is best obtained from the company and found in the Notice of Meeting along with special reports. Of course, advance heralding of liquidating possibilities often appears in news releases as well as in financial reports.

STUBS

Certificates of Participation, Certificates of Contingent Interest, Certificates of Beneficial Interest, liquidation certificates, and receipts all have one characteristic in common, namely, they are stubs representing a residual interest in a company. Stubs naturally follow a discussion of liquidations since, in effect, they frequently arise out of a liquidation.

It is usual for stubs to have a fixed, or calculable, asset value. The release of these assets is the corporate event establishing the profit. Then the main influence upon a stub would be time, that is, how long will it be until the assets are distributed? Since the stub would be available for less than its estimated ultimate value, we equate the indicated profit to the length of time the money may be invested in the stub to arrive at percentage-wise profit. Stubs may have "windfall" possibilities not indicated in the early period of their existence. This may come into being as a result of favorable tax litigation or obscure assets brought to light late in the liquidation procedure.

Unlike ordinary securities, purchasable in one standard way directly from the seller, stubs may be acquired as well by direct purchase in the securities market through the issuing company before consummation of "something doing" creating the stub. Stubs purchased in the securities market generally are low priced, reflecting major distribution of the liquidating company's assets. However, acquiring stubs via purchase through the issuing company is a special situation procedure expedited as follows: We refer to the liquidation of American Viscose mentioned earlier for our example.

Special Situations in Securities

Immediately prior to the effective date of the exchange offer, AVC was priced around $80, while the package had an indicated value in excess of $82 a share. Therefore, at this latest time for participation, one could have purchased AVC, sold the Monsanto Chemical shares, and retained the Certificates of Participation at little or no cost. Since the Certificates (or stubs) had a market value around $2.00 a share at that time, creation of stubs offered an opportunity to participate in a residual situation, having possibilities of potentially greater value. The first liquidating payment totaled $3.00 a share, while a final payment is expected.

Steps to consider when investing in a stub include the following:

1. Find the net value of remaining fixed assets. This may be obtained from the company or derived from financial analysis of the balance sheet.
2. Identify the stub with its origin for a clue to the kind of situation to expect. This may disclose its duration period and ultimate worth.

We list a few stubs showing origin, company of issue, and "something doing," or corporate event that brought the stub into being:

Origin	Company	Corporate Action
Tax Reserve	AVC	Tax Refund Claim
Residual Assets	British Columbia Pr.	Liquidation
Tax Refund	Citadel Industries	Liquidation
Residual Assets	Hayes Holding	Merger
Residual Assets	Holyoke Shares	Liquidation
Residual Assets	LNC	Liquidation
Residual Assets	Peabody Coal	Acquisition
Residual Assets	Delhi Taylor Oil	Liquidation
Reversionary Claim	Atlanta & West Point Railway	Recapitalization
Reversionary Claim	Western Railway of Alabama	Recapitalization

SPIN-OFFS AND DIVESTITURES

Special situation spin-offs and divestitures, categories closely allied with liquidations, are taking on more significance for trading possibilities in light of increased activity arising partially from government actions causing divestments of businesses by large enterprises and activity of conglomerates disposing of certain assets acquired via acquisition or merger. Ling-Temco-Vought used this method to raise cash for further acquisitions when it disposed of its bank and insurance holdings.

A spin-off has liquidation characteristics to the extent that assets are distributed. Unlike liquidations, profit possibilities may be present in both the parent as well as the divested company. Experience shows that in spin-off situations, the newly released company often has greater value marketwise than was attributed to it as a subsidiary. This is clearly demonstrated in the spin-off of Screen Gems by Columbia Pictures.

Through a "rights" offering, a portion of Screen Gems shares was spun off to Columbia stockholders at $9 a share. Creation of a public market for Screen Gems stock brought to light hidden earning power around the time of issuance, reflected in the shares rising to the $18 level. In view of Screen Gems' rise in value, Columbia's shares developed characteristics found in discount situations, since it had retained 89% of Screen Gems' capitalization, equal to about $27.50 a share, when Columbia was priced around $28 to $29 a share. Market recognition of Screen Gems' value contributed to a rise in Columbia's shares from a low of $23 in February to $34 a share by the end of March of the same year.

In another illustration, Grinnell Corp. was ordered by the Justice Department to file a plan for divestiture of three companies in which it held controlling interest. Under the divestiture plan, Grinnell shareholders received 1 share of American District Telegraph, 1/4 share of Holmes Electric, and 1/10 share of Automatic Fire Alarm for each Grinnell share held. The Grinnell shares rose more than 100 points during the waiting period for distribution of the package. This rise reflected the market as well as the investor's estimate of the value of the shares to be spun off. Such market action reflected the investor's belief in "the parts being worth more than the whole." This is a cornerstone approach to special situation investing in "spin-offs." Grinnell as a divestiture then, afforded hidden assets' potential arising from values in companies divested, as well as their worth to the parent company as disclosed by their operations.

At the time of the divestiture, the package being distributed did have a market value of approximately $100, while the parent company's shares were also priced around the $100 mark.

Profit Potential in Spin-Offs

The profit potential in spin-offs lies in analysis of the company to be divested. For this, we refer to our master financial analytical procedure outlined earlier in this chapter. The profit potential would arise from (a) anticipation of economic benefits expected to accrue to the spun off corporation upon release from parental restraints, and (b) marketwise seasoning of securities to be spun off during the period preceding the spin-off.

Background of Spin-Offs

The federal government, through its mediums the Bank Holding Company Act, Public Utility Holding Company Act, and antitrust cases initiated by the Justice Department, are points of origin for spin-offs.

DuPont's divestment of its General Motors' stock is a classic of the industry.

Situations where divestitures could arise are:

United Shoe Machinery. News items indicate that the Justice Department may press its efforts to break up this company into two competing companies.

General Foods. According to a news release, it may divest its SOS Co. in compliance with an FTC order.

El Paso Natural Gas. Was ordered by the US Supreme Court to divest itself of the 1,600-mile Pacific Northwest Pipeline system that was merged into El Paso. El Paso proposed formation of a new company whose stock would be offered to El Paso stockholders. The plan contained four alternate methods: a single distribution to holders of El Paso common stock; distribution to El Paso stockholders over a three-year period; sale of stock under a rights offering to El Paso stockholders; or a single distribution as part of the company's stock and a rights offering of the remainder to El Paso stockholders. However, the plan may be discarded in view of the decision of a federal district judge making final his order selecting Colorado Interstate to buy El Paso's interest in the pipeline for $100 million. This would by-pass distribution to stockholders.

Gulf & Western Industries. Stated that at an appropriate time the company may spin off its real estate developments and sell part of the stock to the public. This conglomerate acquired extensive real estate holdings through its acquisitions including New Jersey Zinc, Paramount Pictures, E. W. Bliss, and South Puerto Rico Sugar.

SBIC of New York. Solved an internal struggle by splitting into two parts. Under the plan approved by directors, SBIC of New York would form a subsidiary, Creative Capital, that would assume 45% of the assets and liabilities of the company. Shares of the new concern would then be spun off to stockholders of SBIC of New York.

Federal Trade Commission. Charged that Kennecott Copper's acquisition of Peabody Coal violated the anti-merger section of the Clayton Antitrust Act. If the hearings find the acquisition illegal, Kennecott would be required to divest all the plants, equipment, and other facilities acquired from Peabody.

The Federal Trade Commission also ordered ABEX Corp. to divest its S.K. Wellman unit of Bedford, Ohio.

New England Electric System. A holding company controlling 12 subsidiaries. As a result of a decision by the U.S. Supreme Court upholding the Securities & Exchange Commission order, the company will have to divest itself of its gas properties, all of which are located in Massachusetts. This is compliance with provisions of the

Holding Company Act of 1935. That era revealed great value in hidden assets of utility holding companies through their ownership of operating units whose activities had not been publicized.

The spin-off procedure may be traced to the many mergers and acquisitions in recent years. Frequently, after marriage, a corporation may find it has an asset not fitting within the scope of the company's activities. This may lead to spinning off the property or subsidiary. Profit possibilities would arise mainly in the divested asset.

APPRAISALS

Appraisal situations find their genesis in rights of stockholders. The goal of an appraisal is to obtain a better price for a security than the pending offer affords. Thus, the appraisal route is the dissenters' expression of their rights. Stockholders' rights are important and defined by law as well as the corporation's charter. A request for an appraisal, or "fair value," is the sole area where action is initiated by the stockholder. The procedure for requesting a fair value for one's securities is defined in the Notice of Meeting as well as in prospectuses.

Stockholders' Rights and Obligations

The right to request an appraisal, or "fair value," for one's securities is not inherent in every administrative corporate act. When the stockholder resorts to this right, he is obligated to sell his shares at the appraised or agreed-upon price.[1] In turn, the corporation is obligated to pay the appraised price. To preserve his rights as a stockholder, the share owner must exercise his right to vote. A penalty for not voting may be forfeiture of privilege to request an appraisal. When establishing a demand for an appraisal, a usual requirement is submission to the corporation of written objection to proposed corporate action. The time for such filing is indicated in the Notice of Meeting.

---

[1] Recent court decisions have followed a pattern of basing appraisal suit settlements on market prices of shares around time of consummation of the corporate action. This inadequate procedure has restrained use of the appraisal procedure, awaiting such time when a more equitable view of securities holders' rights will obtain.

Stockholder Creates the Profit Potential

Estimating a value for a security is more significant in an appraisal situation than other investments because calculated values must be justified. Support for estimated values may have to be presented to various persons whose thinking in relation to values may differ materially from yours. Those whom you must convince include:

1. *The corporation*, where you as a stockholder have initiated the dispute. Obviously, the company knows the extent to which it will go toward compromising, since in its preferred position, it knows the worth of the stock.
2. *Selected appraisers, arbitrators, or a court.* The first contact is with the corporation. Failure to arrive at an agreement may result in security holders petitioning the court to have the value of their shares determined by appraisal, subject to confirmation or determination by the court.
3. *Fellow investors* using similar criteria in evaluating the worth of a security is a simple matter. However, to convince those using dissimilar criteria creates problems. As a special situation investor, strong emphasis is placed on cash, fixed assets, earning power, and relative position in the industry. With these criteria, your case could be established without reference to market prices of the securities. On the other hand, a referee, judge, or jury unfamiliar with professional investors' techniques would find merit to the argument that a security's worth should approximate[2] (a) the market price on date of consummation of corporate action, or (b) the market prices for the security over a reasonable period of time.

Hazards associated with appraisals are:
1. Legal request for appraisal incurs risk of loss of control of securities. This means you may not sell such securities until

---

[2] A common characteristic of an appraisal is settlement out of court. Since such proceedings are confidential, there is a scarcity of statistical data on compromises. Thus, it is difficult for an investor to know the price another security holder received for his stock.

Special Situations in Securities

released by (a) settlement of claim, or (b) permission of defending company to withdraw the appraisal request.
2. A locked-in position may be costly when delayed by slow court procedure or purposeful delaying tactics by the company.
3. The court appraiser's verdict may compel settlement at less than the company offer.
4. Dissenters or those who request appraisals must be prepared to press their claim through litigation, a procedure that can be costly.

As one can see, an appraisal situation is primarily an independent action, since each appraisal request must be made individually. However, by judicious checking, one may find other dissenters with whom to join forces. This would not only reduce costs but also strengthen the position.

TENDERS

A tender is an invitation offering securities for sale subject to specified terms. The security holder is permitted to offer securities at a stated time and price. The price should be more advantageous than that obtainable in the market to be of value to the security holder. A tender invitation qualifies as a special situation when it affords safety as well as potential profit.

A special situation investor would make use of a tender invitation arising under the following conditions: (a) when a substantial amount of a specific security is wanted by a purchaser at a specific time, (b) when a company is in partial liquidation and uses the tender medium to acquire its own shares, (c) when a merger/acquisition and reorganization is being expedited.

A standard use of the tender medium is for redemption of securities under charter provisions, known as sinking fund tenders. In the main, this applies to bonds. Informed investors have made use of this procedure by purchasing the security at a price below the stated sinking fund price, the intention being to await sale of the security through the sinking fund tender. Should the security be accepted at the tender invitation, then a profit would be made. If that security were not accepted, then it would be held until the next period when the sinking fund would be activated.

As special situation investors, we are interested in current tenders because the indicated tender price is higher than the market price of the security. There are avenues of obtaining maximum background information to determine whether or not to participate. Fundamentally, we want to know:

1. Will my securities be accepted?
2. What is my investment position should the securities not be accepted? Answers to these questions, as well as working through a step-by-step procedure of a typical tender, are presented in the following analytical study of Warner Bros. Pictures' tender invitation. We use this particular example because it affords answers to the five main questions underlying most tenders.

Warner Bros. Pictures' tender invitation was designed to reacquire $20 million of its stock at prices not exceeding $28.50 a share. Prior to the announcement, the stock moved from $23.50 to the $26 level. The tender invitation stated that offerings would be accepted at lowest prices and that transactions would be consummated about two months hence. The company's price limitation, combined with the amount of money to be expended, suggested the following question-and-answer approach:

1. *What percentage* of the outstanding shares could $20 million purchase? This gauges the likelihood of stock offerings being accepted. If the percentage is large, then it is likely the stock would be accepted. Based on a price of $28 a share, the $20 million could purchase 710,000 shares, equal to 25% of the outstanding stock. This is a large percentage for a company to purchase.
2. *What is the attitude* of large stockholders? Members of the Warner family indicated they would tender 100,000 shares at

Special Situations in Securities

$27.50. However, a large holder representing almost 40% of the outstanding stock said no offering would be made.

3. Could the tender invitation exhaust the entire $20 million? To consume the $20 million, 50% of the free stock would have to be tendered. It would be difficult to obtain such a large percentage.
4. *What is the risk* if the tender is not accepted? Generally, the stock would decline to a level around the pre-tender time. However, in this case, the possibility of a substantial reduction in the number of outstanding shares could exert a stabilizing influence. This premise proved true, since the stock moved to $29.50 subsequent to expiration of the tender.
5. *Is the stock worth owning?* Examination of the stock via our master financial analysis supported an affirmative approach. This combined with favorable aspects of the tender, and indications that dividends sufficient to pay for use of one's money while waiting would accrue, reaffirmed the tender invitation as worth pursuing.

Warner Bros. Pictures purchased nearly $18 million of its stock at prices up to $28.50 a share. Our illustrative purchases were offered at prices ranging from $28.25 to $28.49 per share. Since investments were not held for more than three months, the rate of return ranged from 36% to 80%.

Tenders offer more than one trading method for participation. Unlike our previous example, where the trading procedure was to purchase shares and sell for cash, some tenders offer securities as means of payment. This, of course, affords an opportunity to hedge by selling against securities to be received. The following example of Mississippi River Fuel's use of tender to acquire Missouri Pacific RR Class A shares illustrates this.

Terms of the exchange offer provided for 1 1/3 shares of Mississippi River Fuel common stock for each share of Missouri Pacific A. The offer was contingent upon receiving 900,000 shares. Since Mopac A was priced around $44 a share and Mississippi River at

$34.50, a spread of 1 7/8 points was present. This type of situation offers two trading opportunities. One is to purchase Mopac A and wait until the effective date of the tender. The second method would be to sell short a portion of the Mississippi stock that one would hope to get, thereby establishing a hedge position. Should market fluctuations be favorable, it might be possible to close out the hedge position prior to the tender date, or await the tender date and, after finding out the number of your shares accepted by Mississippi, sell the residual Mopac A in the market.

The Glen Alden tender invitation for Schenley shares offered a 6% return over a three- to four-week period of investment. At the time the registration was approved, Schenley stock was priced around $53, thereby making the package cost for 1 1/2 shares approximately $80.00. Terms of the tender offered $100 principal amount of 6% debentures plus cash of $13 in exchange for 1 1/2 shares of Schenley. This package had a value of $85 when the plan became effective. Thus, a profit of $5 could have been obtained against each $80 investment, equivalent to a return of 6% on the money.

Capital gains obtained from tender invitations without exercising the tender offer. This procedure could have been followed in the case of the Pacific Vegetable Oil Co. A tender offer to buy 75,000 shares of Pacific Vegetable Oil stock at $17 a share was made public and remained in effect for two weeks. The stock was priced around the mid-$14 level at the time of the offer and moved up two points on the news.

A notable observation about tenders is that companies utilizing this method for acquisition of securities make still further use of the tender. Consequently, an investor could think in terms of offering his securities at the initial tender and for that portion not accepted await a future tender invitation. This occurred in Eastern Gas & Fuel, another tender invitation, where terms provided for an exchange of stock for stock, i.e., 1 share of Norfolk & Western common for each 2 shares of Eastern Gas & Fuel common. Eastern Gas & Fuel was priced around $41.25, and Norfolk & Western at $90.50. This equaled a spread of 4 points. Since the tender invitation was limited in number of shares to be accepted, the probability of a carry-over was indicated. The result of the tender was that 68 1/2% of the stock offered was accepted. This meant that for each 100 Eastern Gas offered at the tender, the stockholder received 34 shares of Norfolk & Western, as well as having 32 shares of Eastern Gas returned to him. Later on, Eastern Gas & Fuel again offered a similar exchange. At the time, Eastern Gas was priced at $52 and Norfolk & Western at $109. Since the exchange terms provided for 1/2 share of Norfolk for each Eastern, a spread of 2 1/2 points was present. This is another example of recurring opportunities in tenders. Then later that year, Eastern Gas & Fuel agreed to purchase 109,264 shares of its own stock from a group of stockholders at $89 a share. The stock was priced around $82 the day prior to the announcement. We can see that in the Eastern Gas & Fuel case, use of repetitive tenders to "buy in" the company's own shares was the clue to desirability of the stock for capital gains potential.

A TRADING PROCEDURE TO BE USED IN SOME TENDER INVITATION SITUATIONS

A tender offer by Schenley Industries to purchase 1 million of its own shares at $32 a share created unusual market reactions arising from an injunction granted to a stockholder. This legal action delayed consummation and caused wide fluctuations in stock prices. Nevertheless, despite adverse conditions, it was possible to purchase Schenley stock after the company's formal announcement to accept tenders of its shares and create a profit for the investor. The impact of the tender, if fully accepted, would remove almost 25% of the floating supply of stock from the market. In light of the high percentage of the outstanding stock to be purchased, an investor could anticipate having approximately half of his tendered shares accepted. Thus, he could buy Schenley around $29 and be reasonably certain of selling a good part of his holdings at $32. Then, upon termination of the tender, he could sell that portion of shares not accepted. In effect, the company accepted only 42 1/2% of all stock tendered. This was disappointing and unusual. Furthermore, it required a larger number of shares to be sold in the market than had been anticipated. Nevertheless, when the tender was consummated, the residual stock could have been sold around the $29 level. While this sale would result in a small loss, the net result of the transaction would be profitable, since the profit made on the shares tendered would be greater than the loss on the residual shares.

OVER-SUBSCRIPTIONS

Over-subscriptions are special situation categories offering "something for nothing." Many investors permitted this "gift" to go by the board simply from being unaware of this by-way trading procedure. Stockholders in a company have an excellent opportunity for profit where an over-subscription privilege has been offered.

Over-subscriptions come about from a "rights" privilege from the company in offering additional shares to its stockholders. The oversubscription privilege is the company's offer to *those holders* who have exercised their privilege of subscribing to additional shares to participate in distribution of the remaining unsubscribed portion on a pro rata basis.

As we know, subscription offerings last about two weeks. Profits arise as a result of shares allotted with participation in the oversubscription at the basic subscription price. Since the basic price is below market price, we make the difference by selling shares when allotted, or we can own low-cost shares should we decide to hold. For example: company A offers to its stockholders rights to subscribe to shares at $20 a share, carrying with it the privilege to participate in any unsubscribed shares. The market price of shares at expiration of the rights is $23 a share. This equals a spread of $3 a share and harbors potential profit in over-subscription allotment. We know rights have negotiable value related to the spread between the subscription price and market price of the securities. As a stockholder of company A, we subscribe to our additional stock at $20, at the same time indicating a desire to participate in the over-subscription according to stated

Special Situations in Securities

terms, disclosing limitations on the number of shares we may subscribe to. After expiration of the rights, we are notified of allotment of 50 shares in our over-subscription, meaning we can purchase 50 shares at $20 a share from the company. If we so desire, we may sell at $23 and establish a gross profit of approximately $150. In effect, we have received a free privilege to buy 50 shares at $20, whereas public purchasers would have had to pay $20 plus the cost of the rights through subscription, or $23 in the market. The cost of the rights equals the $3 spread.

How to Calculate the Value of a Right

A point to remember is that each share is entitled to one right. If 10 rights are required to purchase one share of stock at $20 and the stock is selling at $22, then the value of the right is 20¢. We obtain the value of a right by subtracting $20, the subscription price, from $22 and dividing the remainder of $2 by 10, the number of rights needed to purchase one share. Should our calculations take place before the ex-dividend date, then we add 1 right for the dividend and divide $2 by 11, resulting in a value of 18¢ per right.

MERGERS AND ACQUISITIONS

The terms "merger" and "acquisition" frequently are used interchangeably. A merger is a combination of two or more business enterprises into a single unit through transfer of properties to one surviving corporation. A merger permits pooling of assets and operations of the combining corporations.

Special situation profit opportunities are present in securities of the corporation to be absorbed. Merger plans are processed via an exchange of shares. Thus, in mergers, relative values come into play reflecting exchange of securities. This is so because share prices of the dominant company become the key to profit potentials.

The relationship of stock of the company to be merged compared to the value of shares to be received in exchange harbors the profits. Securities of a company to be absorbed would be the buying medium,

since shares to be received would have a higher value than those of the company being merged. The securities subject to the exchange offer two available trading procedures for establishing a position in a merger situation:
1. Purchase the undervalued or lower-priced security, await the exchange date, then sell the securities so received.
2. Purchase securities of the company to be merged and establish a hedge position by selling "short" securities to be received under the merger plan.

For example: Scott Paper and S.D. Warren Co. announced an agreement to merge. Terms called for Warren stockholders to receive 2.05 shares of Scott Paper common for each Warren common. Based on the then-current prices of $47.75 for Warren common and $28 for Scott Paper common, each share of Warren had an indicated value of $57.40. The procedure for the hedge position is:

Buy 100 shares of S.D. Warren @ $47.75	($4,775)
Sell short 205 shares Scott Paper @ $28	$5,740
Gross proceeds	$965
The gross profit shows a return of 20%.	

Directors of Montgomery Ward & Co. and Container Corp. of America approved the plan for combination of the two companies. Terms called for formation of a new company, "Marcor Inc.," in which Montgomery Ward shareholders would receive 1 share of the new company for each share held. For each share of Container Corp. common, shareholders would receive 1 share of new preferred, having a convertible privilege of 1 for 1, thus making the exchange equivalent to a share-for-share basis. Since a spread of 5 points was present and the stockholders meeting was but three months away, a hedge position could have been established:

Buy 100 shares Montgomery Ward @ $32	($3,200)
Sell short 100 shares Container Corp. @ $37	$3,700
Gross spread	$500

Special Situations in Securities

The short position would be closed out by delivery of the new preferred stock or by converting the new preferred into common and then making delivery.

A *partial hedge* position that offered a substantial profit was inherent in the White Consolidated-Blaw-Knox Co. merger. The indicated price that White offered for Blaw-Knox was based on a price of $59 for Blaw-Knox common as compared with the market price of $44. This was equal to a spread of 15 points.

Terms called for an exchange of 1/2 share of White Consolidated common and 0.55 of a share of its $3.00 series $50 par preferred stock for each share of Blaw-Knox common. Since Blaw-Knox was priced around $44 and White common at $72.50, the hedge procedure would be as follows:

Buy 100 shares of Blaw-Knox @ $44	($4,400)
Sell short 50 shares of White common @ $72.50	$3,625
Residual invested in 0.55 White preferred	($775)
At the time merger is effective, sell:	
55 White preferred @ $40	$2,200
This creates a gross profit of	$1,425

Since the merger was consummated within three months, the rate of return would be better than 30%.

During the period the position is open, dividends on the shares of the company purchased are credited to the investor's account, while dividends paid by the company where a short position exists are charged against the investor's account.

ACQUISITIONS

An acquisition is consummated upon obtaining controlling interest of a company, thereby making the parent company (the acquirer) the dominant factor in the combined enterprise. Acquisitions may not require approval by stockholders of both companies, since acquiring facilities would generally come within the scope of administrative functions. Furthermore, acquisitions can be achieved by sole activities of a single company.

Unlike a direct sale of a company, in an acquisition, the acquired company does not necessarily lose its identity, although the business is controlled by the acquiring company. Special situation profit potential is in the value of outstanding securities of the company to be acquired in relation to the offered price. The special situation approach is similar to liquidations, since we deal with a set price. Channels used by companies to process an acquisition are:

1. Purchase of shares in the securities market.
2. An offer to stockholders to exchange securities.
3. Cash payment offered to stockholders for the outstanding securities of the company to be acquired.

Since the potential profit is in the price, the medium used to acquire the company will influence the selection of the special situation trading procedure. An offer to exchange securities may present hedging opportunities, while cash payment for outstanding securities may present possibilities for profit in discount as well as in percentage-wise return on invested money, reflecting the schedule of cash distributions.

Although investors may not have advance notice of an acquisition, they should not be deterred from participating in the situation, since profit potentials are present from the time the proposed plan becomes public information until the consummation date. This is the discount period indicating uncertainty. The discount (spread) diminishes in direct relation to rate of favorable progress of the plan. On the other hand, a substantial discount sounds the alarm of trouble ahead, a clue to look for opposition.

Serious consideration should be given where opposition is present, since the battle may very well be in stock ownership. Dissension should be represented by a significant percentage of voting stock in order to have influence and meaning. Dissension and doubt about consummation of a plan arising from dissatisfaction with price may be overcome by sweetening the offer. On the other hand, opposition to the acquisition itself may bring about a contest for control, opening opportunities for trading profit potentials.

Merger/Acquisition Investing Approach

After examining a specific merger/acquisition proposal by way of our master analytical and investigative procedure, and we are satisfied consummation of corporate action will be achieved, then the situation is ripe for establishing an investment position. Typical procedures are:

1. Purchase shares of the company to be acquired at *initial public announcement*. The objective in this approach is to obtain profit as a result of the narrowing spread in prices of the participating stocks concerned. This takes place as the merger/acquisition plan approaches realization.
2. Purchase shares of the company to be acquired *near the time stockholders approve the merger/acquisition plan*. This is followed by the waiting period for realization of the plan. At consummation date, dispose of stock received in exchange according to the plan. Purchase may frequently take place within a day or so prior to the stockholders' meeting.
3. Purchase shares *after stockholders have approved the plan but prior to completion of the merger/acquisition*. Establish a hedge position by purchasing securities of the company to be acquired and simultaneously dispose of shares to be received in exchange. Bear in mind that a purchase would be made only when a discount from ultimate worth is present.

The hedging procedure is a vehicle used by stockholders of the company being acquired who do not wish to own stock of the merged company. By anticipating the exchange of shares and disposing of such shares, a fixed price may be obtained. Selling pressure may arise in shares of the parent company reflecting sales by stockholders who awaited actual delivery of the new shares prior to selling. This takes place upon physical consummation of the merger.

An example harboring all three procedures is contained in the acquisition of Majestic Specialties by Genesco.

On the day Majestic Specialties announced plans to join Genesco, it was possible to purchase Majestic stock around $14.50 a share, equal to a discount of approximately 14% from the value in Genesco shares to be received upon consummation of the acquisition. Subsequently, when stockholders of Majestic Specialties approved the plan, Majestic stock was priced around $15 a share. At that point, a discount of approximately 10% was inherent in the situation based on the then-current price of Genesco. At this stage of the development, the investor could have a choice: having purchased Majestic, he could await the exchange date or apply procedure (3) by selling short Genesco shares to be received in exchange for Majestic. This would establish the profit.

A month later, when Majestic shares were officially exchangeable for Genesco shares, the discount had been eliminated, since the stock at that time was priced around $16.75. In view of the short holding period until completion of the acquisition, we can see the rate of return on money invested would be substantial in each procedure.

Where Mergers/Acquisitions May be Found

Mergers/acquisitions arise because of desires to (a) broaden markets, (b) increase growth possibilities, (c) effect economies, and (d) take advantage of substantial tax-loss carry-forward positions. Then too, economic conditions arise wherein a company faced with declining sales seeks association with a larger company. Akin to this area is the "family sell-out," where the founders want to sell or merge to obtain full value for their company as a going concern.

As special situation investors, we would be alert to opportunities in mergers/acquisitions. Litton Industries represents the typical growth-type enterprise, while the food, drug, and tobacco fields are replete with mergers/acquisitions designed to broaden markets. Family sell-outs are avenues arising in separate industries somewhat seasonally or in a fashion-type occurrence. For a long period, the oil

Special Situations in Securities

industry had many acquisitions arising from the sale of family holdings. This trend is noticeable recently in various phases of the soft goods or merchandising industry. Genesco's acquisition of Majestic Specialties is an example of the "family sell-out," reflecting the decision of one family to sell out its dominant control of the company's stock.

The railroad industry is attracting attention at the present time with investor interest in a new concept suggesting that solvent railroads may merge. This is in contrast with an earlier idea that only bankrupt roads may merge. Development of solvent railroad mergers would encourage special situation investor enthusiasm reflecting prospects for substantially higher earnings redounding to the merged roads as a result of elimination of many costs and duplication of services. While quite a few railroad companies have consummated merger plans, there remain a number of interesting situations harboring benefits to be derived from merging. This area includes Northern Pacific Railway and Great Northern Railway; Chicago, Rock Island & Pacific Railroad and Union Pacific Railroad; Rock Island and Chicago and North Western; and Chicago, Milwaukee, St. Paul and Pacific and Chicago and North Western.

Terms of the Chicago, Milwaukee, St. Paul and Pacific/Chicago and North Western offer 0.7 of a share of North Western for each share of Chicago, Milwaukee, St. Paul and Pacific. The market price of $46.50 for St. Paul equals half its indicated merger value.

In the case of the Rock Island merger, proceedings are encountering delays because of the intervention of almost all western carriers. Because of this, Rock Island sells at a wide discount from the indicated value in the merger terms.

REORGANIZATIONS AND RECAPITALIZATIONS

A reorganization in a company is designed to bring about economic relief. It takes place when creditors, who may comprise commercial interests, bondholders and preferred stockholders, hope to regain more through continuation of the business than through liquidation. Reorganization results in elimination of a major portion of burdensome debts. Capitalization changes inherent in reorganization plans afford opportunities for special situation investment.

Profit Opportunities

Profit possibilities arise from differences in the price of the old company's securities and estimated values of new company's securities. The market's evaluation of the new company's securities reflects the significance of the settlement of claims. The impact of this beneficial action may be seen in higher prices for the new than prevailed for the old. Since the old securities are to be exchanged for new securities, then a buyer of the old exchanging them for the new would have profit (arising from the higher prices for new securities).

Why do the new securities command a higher price? The reason is that new securities reflect the approach of consummation of the reorganization plan with renewed hope for the enterprise. The new securities then have qualities inherent in a "going concern." Then too, prospects for future dividends loom brighter and are anticipated in the market prices of the new securities. On the other hand, the old securities are subject to pressure of selling orders by holders who do not care to continue in the reorganized company or wish to dispose of stock because of tax considerations. These influences create a widening of the spread between the old and new securities.

Reorganization Sign Posts

Potential reorganizations are usually visible in the market action of securities well in advance of public announcement of the plan. Therefore, haste is unnecessary when examining a plan, since revisions are quite usual. Highlights and the schedule of proceedings leading to a reorganization follow:

1. Financial difficulties or insolvency of a company.
2. Preliminary efforts to continue functioning.
3. Presentation of plans to re-establish the company.

Special Situations in Securities

4. Agreement on a reorganization plan by authorized persons or groups.
5. Approval of plan by regulatory bodies, A reorganization may need approval of: the federal courts; the SEC, ICC, and FCC; and state agencies; as well as various creditors and securities holders.
6. Formal approval by creditors and securities holders.
7. Certification by the court having jurisdiction.
8. Plan declared operative.
9. Exchange of old securities for securities of the new corporation.

The Profit Potential

The following procedure discloses profit potentials in reorganizations:

1. Estimate a value for new securities based on pro forma financial projections applying our master analytical procedure. Should this result in anticipated prices of new securities being higher than "old securities," then a potential profit is evident. The next step is to investigate probable consummation.
2. Since the reorganization plan is the catalytic agent, our investigation is concerned with "opposition" such as:
   a. How strong are opponents of the plan? What percentage of creditors do they represent?
   b. Does opposition reject the entire plan, or do they seek to improve terms for a specific security issue?

The opposition's progress will be found in published court proceedings, communications of protective committees, news releases by the company, and records of federal and state agencies. Information about opposition will aid in deciding whether or not to invest in the reorganization, since it will disclose news regarding progress and the ultimate duration of reorganization proceedings.

Protective Committees

A reorganization generally leads to formation of protective committees representing each class of creditor and security holder. A committee's recognition stems from the voting strength of the securities they represent. It is not unusual for each class of security to be represented by a committee presenting its own reorganization plan.

Trading Procedures in Reorganizations

One trading procedure in reorganizations is purchase and retention of old securities until consummation, then exchanging for new securities issuable under the reorganization plan. A second method is to establish a hedge position. This is done by purchasing the "old securities" and selling on a "when, as, and if issued" basis the new securities to be received in exchange. The profit is established via the corresponding higher price obtained for new securities in the first instance and the when-issued securities in the hedge position.

"When issued" transactions generally do not come into existence until the reorganization plan approaches the final stage; however, the duration period could be costly in the event of a protracted delay. On the other hand, a delay may offer additional opportunities to enter the situation. This would be desirable where securities are accruing interest during the waiting period.

The "Money Stage"

This period is known as the "money stage," since a trading profit of but 2% is all that may remain at this point. Nevertheless, 2% earned in a month is equivalent to a per annum rate of return of 24%. This phase of the reorganization takes place at realization, the date established for exchanging securities. The 2% spread merely reflects technical processing in consummating the reorganization.

Railroad Reorganizations

We draw upon history for trading procedures developed to meet specific securities trading conditions. These procedures have application today in various aspects of securities trading, namely liquidations, spin-offs, reorganization/recapitalizations, and divestitures. A feature of the railroad and utility reorganization periods was the use of an arbitraging procedure by investors.

The following table presents an arbitrage work sheet. Reference will also be made to this tabulation later. The tabulation shows the procedure for establishing an arbitrage position wherein we purchased Denver & Rio Grande 4% bonds and sold "when issued" securities as a hedge against purchase. The net spread of $1,082.47 is the indicated profit materializing when the reorganization would consummate. A feature of the arbitrage/hedge procedure was its application for creating a long position in a selected new security at a price substantially below the prevailing market. This could be accomplished by purchase of the senior security (in our example, the Denver & Rio Grande 4%'s) to be exchanged for a "package"[3] of "when issued" securities forthcoming under the reorganization plan.

The procedure is to apply the anticipated profit created by the arbitrage/hedge against cost of the selected security, in our example, the preferred stock. As noted in the example, the net spread shows a profit of $1,082.47 based on a sale of all securities to be received. However, by selling all but one class of security, the proceeds are automatically applied against the cost of the unsold security.

---

3   A package is an assortment of securities issued as a single group, i.e., bonds and preferred and common stock issued as a unit in exchange for a first mortgage bond.

DENVER & RIO GRANDE WESTERN RAILROAD CO.

Arbitrage Work Sheet

The federal district court approved the ICC plan for reorganization, and final consummation is generally expected in about a year.

BUY:	$10,000 Denver & Rio Grande 4%/1936 @ $53	($5,300.00)
	Approximate commission and taxes on completed arbitrage transaction	(65.00)
	Total cost	($5,365.00)
ITEM SELL:	"When-issued" new securities under Plan of Reorganization	
	$3,189.20 Denver & Rio Grande 1st Mortgage 3-4% 1933 @ $87.75	$2,798.52
	$2,170.80 Denver & Rio Grande Income 4 1/2% 2018 @ $56.50	1,226.50
	32.16 shares of Denver & Rio Grande Preferred @ $41.25	1,326.60
	48.24 shares of Denver & Rio Grande Common @ $18.75	904.50
	Accrued interest on above 1st Mortgage bonds (estimated)	191.35
	Proceeds	$6,447.47
	Purchase cost	(5,365.00)
	Net spread	$1,082.47

How to Create Low Cost Preferred or Common Stock

By purchasing the old bond (Denver & Rio Grande 4%/1936) and in turn, selling the first mortgage, income bonds, and common stock (items A, B, and D) for a total of $5,120.87, which included interest to be received, your net investment could amount to only $245 ($5,120.87 deducted from $5,365.00), equal to $7.61 per share of new preferred stock.

To create low-cost common stock, the same procedure applies, but we sell items A, B, and C. Total proceeds amount to $5,351.62. Deducting the proceeds from cost, we have a net cost figure of $13.38 for the 48.24 shares to be received. This is equivalent to 28¢ a share. This procedure may be applied to establish a low-cost security wherever more than one security will be issued in a reorganization.

When-Issued Securities

Three main advantages of when-issued securities, when used as a medium for trading, are:

1. The cost of carrying when-issued securities is low. Interest is not charged on the debit balance. Margin requirements are at a minimal level. Since money does not change hands until securities are issued, the margin is applied to protect banks and brokers against possible loss. Should the market price of the when-issued securities decline, then the purchaser is required to maintain the agreed-upon margin by putting up additional funds.

    This "mark to the market" is the difference between the price at which a when-issued security has been sold and the market price at any given time. For example, an investor who sold a when-issued security at $69 could be called upon to deposit 10 points, or $10 a share for each share sold, if, subsequent to his original sale, the security was priced at $79. Correspondingly, a purchaser at $79 would be required to meet the "mark to market" when the security declined to $69.

2. Failure of the reorganization plan to consummate incurs minimal risk to the holder of when-issued contracts, since the contracts are void, limiting the investor's loss to commission charges.

3. When-issued contracts may be used as negotiable instruments. They may be sold at a percentage of the existing profit or loss, prior to the reorganization becoming effective. This procedure is a favorite medium for establishing long-term profits in when-issued situations.

The Denver & Rio Grande work sheet illustrates this procedure. If an investor purchased the 32.16 shares of preferred stock at $41.25 (item C), he in fact entered into a contract with the seller to purchase said shares "when, as, and if issued." Let us assume that more than six months hence, the shares have moved to $50 and the investor wished to establish a profit. If he were to sell the shares, the only way he could do that would be the reverse of his purchase, i.e., sell another contract to deliver 32.16 shares at a price of $50 on a when-issued basis. This might incur margin for an open contract, and he then would have two contracts outstanding. However, he still would not be in a position to close the transaction, since the contracts would be contingent upon consummation of the reorganization plan. His position would show holding one contract to purchase at $41.25 and another to sell at $50.

However, the transaction was simplified by selling his contract, entitling him to stock at $41.25. This contract's value is the difference between $41.25 and the market price of $50, or 8 3/4 points on 32.16 shares, equal to $281.40. Of course, the profit could not be realized until the reorganization was consummated. But, the contract could be sold at a discount from its potential worth, the value being influenced by the stage of the reorganization plan. Via sale of the contract at a discount of 10%, the investor terminated his position and established a net profit of $253.26 immediately.

While the foregoing illustration relates to railroad securities, this approach can be used in other instances where when-issued contracts are in existence.

The *Public Utility Holding Company Act* of 1935 was responsible for many public utility holding companies and consequently created numerous profitable special situation opportunities. Large utility empires were required to divest holdings of operating utility companies.

While the public utility divestment era is old history, certain trading procedures developed during that time may be applied to other investment areas today. Currently, many spin-off corporate actions in commercial enterprises offer opportunities to apply this knowledge.

Columbia Pictures' spin-off of Screen Gems (mentioned earlier) is an example. Recent rumblings arising from antitrust activities in the electrical, cement, food, drug, and other business areas suggest possible breakups of mammoth industrial empires. These are likely areas for profitable investments through divestment procedures (DuPont's program for divestment of General Motors was the forerunner of similar divestiture cases). Public utility divestments validate the concept "the sum of the parts is often greater than the whole." This was substantiated by bringing to light (a) securities values hidden in locked-in subsidiaries, as well as (b) unexplored growth potential often restrained because of absentee management. Subsidiaries' securities values were hidden in the pattern of great-grandfather holding company systems. (*See*, the exhibit of Philadelphia Company and its family of subsidiaries for a typical pattern.) This design has its counterpart in today's widely diversified industrial enterprises.

Conclusion

The importance of reorganizations as a broad field of corporate activities has been recognized by the government (through the SEC) by issuing a booklet listing 125 corporations that have reorganized in recent years. Investors holding "old securities" may find this booklet, "Securities Required to be Exchanged for Cash or Securities," a valuable aid in recovering unexpected assets.

RECAPITALIZATIONS

A recapitalization is an administrative corporate action taking place within the capital structure of a company. In effect, it is a realignment of relationships among outstanding securities of the corporation. Since the capital structure is the focal point of action and sensitive to changes in relationships of securities, the investor's interest (holdings of securities issues) is vulnerable to loss of position. Therefore, the security holder must guard his rights. To protect one's position, the first step is, of course, exercising voting privileges. By his vote, a security holder may oppose a recapitalization plan and may validate a request for a "fair value" for securities.

Significance of Voting in a Recapitalization

To be effective, securities holders, commercial creditors, and others in any way concerned with the capitalization of a corporation are required to approve a recapitalization plan. The percentage of outstanding securities needed for assent in relation to the number of votes controlled by proponents gives a clue to the realization of the plan. In the case of the Virginia Carolina Chemical recapitalization, assent by Allied Chemical, the owner of 20% of voting stock, exerted a dominant influence in bringing about realization of plan. Generally, security holders give greater attention to voting in a recapitalization than in other corporate activities, since the effects of market values can be seen on their securities. An important point to remember is that valuable rights existing in outstanding securities may be lost through supersedence by new issues. This could materially influence security values.

Why Do Recapitalizations Take Place?

The need for and probability of a recapitalization plan materializing is evident long before a company announces it formally. The signs leading to recapitalization are found in maladjusted corporate structures, a result of unbalanced capitalizations from many acquisitions, while other times it may be adverse economic conditions. Significant motives for a recapitalization are:

(A) To carry out a plan of debt adjustment, and
(B) To expedite emergence from financial hardship.

Special Situations in Securities

The following example shows both objectives achieved in a single corporate action. American Electronics completed a recapitalization plan with the aim of putting its net worth and net working capital in the black. The company had liabilities exceeding assets at the time the plan was proposed. The recapitalization was effected by exchange of long-term debentures for convertible preferred stock. As part of the recapitalization plan, short-term notes held by a financial institution were converted into long-term debt. This adjustment reduced annual debt repayment charges by 25%.

A feature of this recapitalization plan is the delayed conversion privilege of the preferred stock at the rate of 10 shares of common for each share of preferred. This privilege opens channels for hedging transactions through purchase of preferred stock and selling short part or all of the common stock into which the preferred could be converted. Then, at the time the conversion privilege is operable, the preferred stock is exchanged for the common and the transaction closed by delivery of the common stock against the short sale.

Profits would rise from the difference in the cost of the preferred and the value of common stock that had been sold short. For example: the preferred stock could have been purchased around $6.00, equal to $600 for 100 shares. At the same time, the common stock was priced around $1.25, equivalent to $1,250 for 1,000 shares. (Bear in mind that each preferred share is exchangeable for 10 common shares.) Fluidity of this type of transaction is reflected in market action of the preferred and common stocks during the waiting period for the conversion privilege to be effective. A rise in the preferred stock without a corresponding rise in the common would permit an investor to sell the preferred and cover his short sale, thus obtaining a profit. On the other side of the coin, a decline in the value of the common without an equivalent erosion of the preferred would permit covering the common stock short sale at a profit and the subsequent sale of the preferred at smaller loss. The net result would be a profit and the subsequent sale of the preferred at a smaller loss. The net result would be a profit.

PHILADELPHIA COMPANY

STANDARD GAS & ELECTRIC COMPANY

STANDARD POWER & LIGHT CORP.

Corporate Chart of the System

<u>Operating Properties</u>

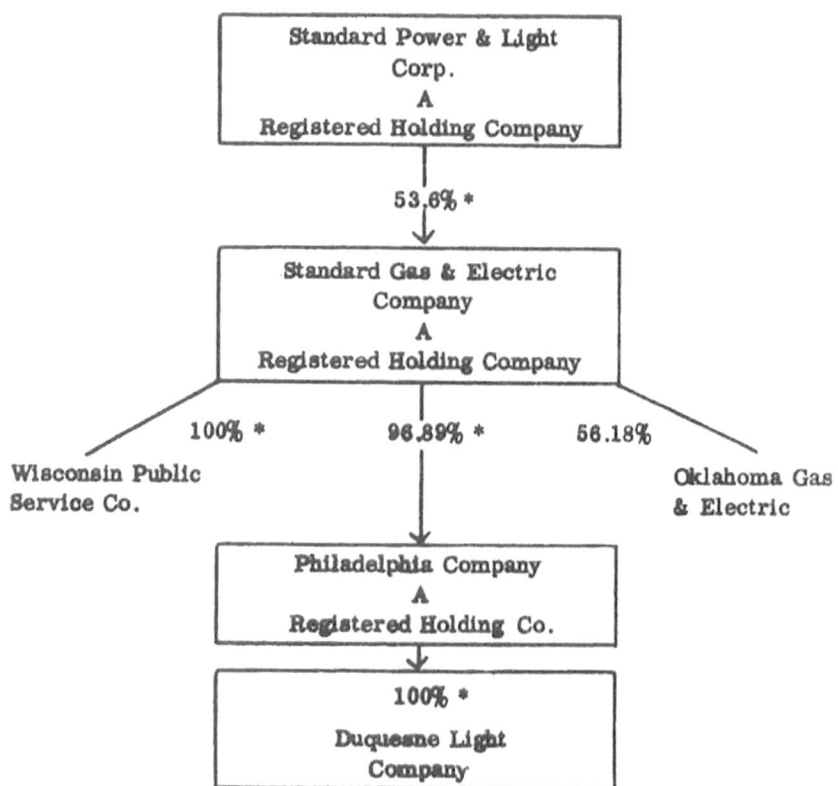

* Indicates percent of common stock owned.

Source: *Fortunes in Special Situations* (Rye, N.Y.: American Research Council, 1961).

(C) *To create a capital gains vehicle* for long-term investors. Ling-Temco-Vought consummated a major recapitalization program that combined the prospect of cash savings that could reach upward to $100 million over a 10-year period and also offer stockholders a vehicle for long-term capital gains. Under the plan, shareholders could exchange their common and Series A preferred stock for a new class of preference stock. The latter would be convertible into common at 0.75 shares and rise to 1.5 shares by 1980. The new preference stock would be non-callable until 1977 and callable thereafter at liquidating value. The preference stock would, in the belief of management, be attractive to long-term investors, since no cash dividends would be paid. However, stock dividends of 3% annually were indicated. Upon sale of the preference stock received as dividends, taxes would be computed at capital gains rates.

(D) *To clear accumulated dividend arrears.* The H. C. Bohack recapitalization was designed to clear dividend arrears by offering an exchange of $120 at 6% convertible debentures for each share of preferred. A feature of this offer is the payment of debenture interest in common stock. Reflecting the significance of the recapitalization, the preferred rose from the $64 level to $99. R. Hoe & Co. approved the plan, aimed at clearing accumulated unpaid dividends and elimination of its Class A stock. The impact of this proposal sent the Class A shares up $4.00 to the $31 level. Under the plan, Class A holders could exchange their stock for common in the ratio of 0.7 shares of common for each Class A share. Since the common was priced at $49, the exchange would be equal to $34 for the Class A. Accumulated unpaid dividends on the Class A amounted to $4.85 a share. The common is restricted as to dividend payments until the Class A is eliminated. The recapitalization is conditioned upon holders of at least 80% acceptance. The Board of Directors approved the plan on September 19th and declared that unexchanged

Class A shares would be redeemed at $16.25 plus accrued dividends.

(E) *To take advantage of lower rates for borrowing money.* Refinancing of high-cost bonds and preferred stock is the area for this activity.

(F) *To elude corporate raiders*: A recent innovation in the use of recapitalization can be seen in the move on the part of Combustion Engineering, which amended its charter to require a corporate raider to have the backing of holders of at least 80% of the outstanding equity shares. The amendment states that an 80% vote of stockholders would be required before a merger or similar transaction can be effected with a corporation that owns more than 10% of any class of the company's equity securities.

(G) *To implement diversification*: The Denver & Rio Grande Western Railroad approved a plan to form a holding company to provide a vehicle for diversification while continuing its status as a major railroad. Such moves have been made by other railroad companies in line with a trend toward greater use of railroad company interests in activities other than railroad properties. The benefits of this type of move have been reflected in higher values for common shares as noted in Chicago & North Western, Santa Fe, and Illinois Industries, all railroads that have formed holding companies.

Types of Recapitalizations

Recapitalization procedures harboring profit possibilities arise in the following circumstances:

1. Creation of new securities used as an exchange medium for old securities. Recent application of this method has been used to implement tax savings by exchanging preferred stock for bonds.
2. Creation of a new class of securities, such as dividend- or interest-bearing certificates to pay debts.

3. Payment of arrears in securities issuable under existing capitalization. In this circumstance, look out for dilution of equity.
4. Payment of arrears in cash. Such action would find speedy response in the securities market.

Analytical Steps

A special situation investment in a recapitalization could be initiated when a plan is under consideration. The investor's procedure would be first to apply our master analytical guide described earlier. The analytical procedure compares old and new capitalizations, viewing each as representing two separate corporations. Therefore, where possible, it would be helpful to construct a balance sheet and earnings statement covering a five-year period: (a) two years earlier, (b) the present year, and (c) two years hence. Then compare earnings, capital assets, and underlying values for each class of security. Special points of interest in recapitalization are:

1. Who proposed the plan? Initiators would be: (a) incumbent management, (b) protective committees, (c) banking groups, and (d) organized opposition to management.
2. Is the plan fair and equitable to all classes of securities?
3. Is the recapitalization necessary or is it a subterfuge?
4. Does the recapitalization relieve stress on the company's structure?
5. What is the voting strength of proponents of the plan?
6. What percentage of voting securities is needed to declare the plan effective?
7. How much time will elapse until voting occurs?
8. Who is the opposition? Why are they opposed? What do they suggest?
9. Who and what do the various committees represent?
10. Does recent market activity show signs of anticipatory purchasing?

CONCLUSION

WE HAVE HIGHLIGHTED the technical aspects of recapitalizations with emphasis on profitable investment areas as well as cautions where capital structures are under consideration. We see varying types of recapitalizations with different procedures for participation. Anticipation of a recapitalization appears in some instances as a likely trading method, while in others, awaiting a confirmation may be wiser. Then, too, the hedging procedure appears as a middle course, since we deal with "old" and "new" securities (or similar securities) traded in the same market. In any event, knowing what to look for and where to find it, combined with judicious application of these trading procedures, could prove most rewarding.

About the Author

MAURECE SCHILLER (1901-1994) began his Wall Street career in 1922, rising to the position of Director of Research at Newburger Loeb & Co., a firm primarily serving individual clients. In 1955, he published the first known book on special situations investing as a field beyond distressed debt, reorganizations and arbitrage, and published four more through 1966. He attended Dartmouth and lived in Larchmont, New York, and Santa Barbara, California.

www.ingramcontent.com/pod-product-compliance
Lightning Source LLC
Chambersburg PA
CBHW031547210526
45464CB00003B/1196